LOVING SOMEONE WITH PTSD

A definitive manual for comprehending, relating to, and knowing
what to anticipate and do when someone you love is
suffering from post- traumatic stress

Angela C. Villela

Table of contents

Chapter 1

Understanding the implications of having a partner with PTSD

You are also impacted by your partner's post-traumatic stress disorder (PTSD). Living with PTSD is difficult, and it may have a negative impact on personal and family connections. You might be hurt by your loved one's distance and moodiness or find it difficult to comprehend why they are acting more irrationally and volatilely. You might also have to shoulder a larger proportion of the household's responsibilities and deal with the frustration of a loved one who won't talk to you. Even worse, PTSD symptoms may result in family-wide issues including drug misuse, job loss, and other issues.

It might be difficult to not take PTSD symptoms personally, but it's crucial to understand that a person with PTSD might not always be in control of their conduct. As a result of their nervous system being "locked" in a state of perpetual alert, your loved one may constantly feel vulnerable and dangerous or be forced to again relive the terrible event. This may result in PTSD symptoms that your loved one can't just decide to turn off, such as rage, impatience, despair, distrust, and others.

With these suggestions, you may assist your loved one in ultimately moving on from the terrible experience and allowing your life together to return to normal. Your loved one's nervous system can get "stuck" with the proper assistance from you and other family and friends, however.

What might your partner do?

Due to the partner's inability to get beyond the trauma, you could feel wounded, alone, or depressed. You could even start to distance yourself or become irritated with your loved one. They could experience stress, pressure, and control. A loved one may feel as if they are always in danger or that they are living in a war zone due to the survivor's symptoms. Living with a spouse who suffers from PTSD may sometimes cause the partner to experience some of the same sensations of having had trauma.

In conclusion, someone who experiences trauma may exhibit several typical responses. Those close to the survivor are impacted by these emotions. The majority of the changes might show up in;

#Intimacy

This suggests intimacy within a bond that may be emotional or sexual, and often both.
Living with a partner who has PTSD may have an impact on intimacy in relationships if they exhibit particular symptoms, such as:

lack of enthusiasm for rewarding pursuits
adverse self-perception
an emotional disconnect or a sense of being emotionally distant from others
A person with PTSD could feel the urge to be intimate with their spouse yet struggle to do so because of fear or inability.

#Sexual desire

It might be difficult to predict how PTSD will impact your romantic relationship.

The kind of trauma that first set off your PTSD may also determine if and how it impacts the two of you.

In situations of sexual assault or trauma, sex may rise to the top of the list of things they avoid.

Your partner could find it difficult to trust you or to feel secure in a sexually intimate setting as a result of this sort of trauma. This is an organic response to trauma.

Research also shows that trauma may lead to hypersexuality in certain situations. Despite being a contentious subject, hypersexuality is often characterized as the emergence of difficult-to-control obsessive sexual practices.

Your partner's sex life may also be affected by other PTSD symptoms, such as:

- adverse self-perception
- absence of sleep
- minimal sex desire
- feeling remote
- hypervigilance that makes relaxing difficult
- lack of enthusiasm for pleasurable experiences

This might be the cause of your partner's lack of interest in or dread of having sex with you despite how much they care for you.

#Communication

Every relationship has to have open communication. Your relationship with your partner may suffer if it becomes difficult for them.

Angry outbursts and impatience are two PTSD symptoms that might occur. Then, your spouse can react to you in a manner that you don't understand, are afraid of, or dislike.

How they handle disagreements may also be impacted by other symptoms, such as trouble-solving issues.

Your spouse could get excessively worried and overwhelmed with even the shortest conversation, which might prevent you from effectively expressing yourself.

They may also have times when they just want to be left alone and don't want to talk at all. Establishing connections may be hampered by your partner's incapacity to communicate.

#Negative shifts in thought and mood

Negative shifts in thought and mood might manifest as the following symptoms:

- negative perceptions of oneself, others, or the world
- a lack of optimism for the future
- Memory issues, such as forgetting crucial details of the traumatic incident
- Keeping tight ties is difficult.
- feeling cut apart from friends and relatives
- Absence of enthusiasm for things you previously liked
- having trouble feeling good feelings
- a lack of emotional response

Arousal symptoms, often known as altered bodily and emotional responses, might include:

- being prone to being surprised or alarmed
being always alert for danger
  - Self-destructive conduct, such as binge drinking or speeding
  - difficulty sleeping
  - difficulty focusing
  - Anger flare-ups, irritability, or violent conduct
  - overwhelming shame or remorse

Understanding these indicators is essential because it will help you determine which portion of your partner's attention they require from you the most.

While PTSD affects everyone differently, the following are some things your spouse could be going through:

#1- Flashbacks

People with PTSD often replay specific events from their terrible experiences. They can have nightmares or flashbacks to the actual incident. Flashbacks may be brought on by a variety of circumstances, such as a symbolic reminder of the incident. For instance, it may be a word, a date, a sound, a fragrance, or more. They could have persistent, bothersome flashbacks to the incident. PTSD may have physical effects in addition to mental ones. When having a flashback, a person with PTSD could experience bodily symptoms like pain or nausea.

#2- Avoidance

Trauma has been experienced by people with PTSD, and they may try to avoid the distressing emotions that come with it. Avoidance comes in a variety of forms. Alcohol or drugs may be used by PTSD sufferers as a coping strategy. They could isolate themselves from their loved ones or friends, or they might steer clear of anything that brings back bad memories. They could experience emotional or bodily numbness or even a sense of body disconnection.

#3 - Being "tense"

It's possible for persons with PTSD to have signs of anxiety. They may feel startled, jumpy, or too alert. They can have problems focusing or falling asleep.

#4: Complicated Beliefs and Feelings

People with PTSD face tough ideas and emotions. They can believe that no one can relate to them or that no one can be trusted. They could feel guilty, unhappy, or ashamed of the terrible occurrence, or they might place responsibility on themselves. Even if there is no connection between a circumstance or location and the traumatic incident, they may feel unsafe in particular situations or locations.

I keep emphasizing this because you must make a sincere effort to envision how your spouse feels since you will never really comprehend it. Even while you are putting out a lot of work that will undoubtedly be valued in the future, you must also realize that your spouse is not enjoying how they are feeling. Indeed, being a partner to someone who is experiencing PTSD is not easy, but it is also not enjoyable for them.

Chapter 2

Relationship- based causes of PTSD

The impact of PTSD from any source, including war or a natural tragedy, may be felt strongly in a person's relationships.

However, relationship-based trauma often results in PTSD, which may make it harder to feel at ease in future relationships.

PTSD's relationship-based causes include:

Sexual assault or abuse

Immediately after a sexual attack, a victim often experiences significant levels of anguish. Being abused may cause trauma that results in feelings of dread, rage, guilt, anxiety, and grief. For some individuals, the stigma attached to sexual assault may be embarrassing or shameful.

Additionally, there is a higher chance that those who have experienced sexual assault may have PTSD symptoms including nightmares and intrusive thoughts. They may mistrust other individuals and feel as if they must continually be on guard or worry about danger.

Psychological Abuse

One person manipulating another emotionally is referred to as emotional abuse. It may take the form of statements and deeds meant to offend, dominate, terrify, or isolate.

Taking away your freedom and privacy; separating you from loved ones, work, and activities; expecting to always be aware of your whereabouts and activities; frightening you with anger; posing a threat to you and those you care about; and humiliating and belittling you are some examples of emotional abuse.
Psychological trauma, such as emotional abuse, may have an equivalent effect on the nervous system as physical trauma.

The Demise of a Loved one

Throughout their life, people have many ties with their family, friends, colleagues, and neighbors. We have the strongest bonds with the people we love because they shape who we are. They are a part of who we are and can change us for the better or worse. As a result, losing a loved one may result in a variety of psychological problems, including PTSD, especially if the loss was sad and unexpected.

We are aware that following the passing of a loved one, survivors often endure despair or anxiety. We rarely consider them to have posttraumatic stress disorder.

disorder (PTSD), but it can also occur, particularly following a tragic death.

Kidnapping

A terrible occurrence, like being kidnapped, might leave you with post-traumatic stress disorder (PTSD). During a traumatic event, you think that your life or others' lives are in danger. You can experience fear or the impression that you have no control over the world around you.

Prisoner of war
Military personnel who experience combat-related stress, such as watching others murdered, seeing corpses on the ground, or getting threats to their life, are more likely to acquire PTSD.

However, the trauma that occurs not just during a battle but also during training or even in times of peace may result in PTSD.

<u>How PTSD Affects Partners in Relationships</u>

People who are intimately involved with PTSD sufferers may experience their symptoms and emotions as a consequence of the interaction. These may consist of:

Sympathy
Though this is normal, you might start to feel sorry for your partner. However, if you express this sympathy too much, your partner might mistake it for pity.

Worry and fear
If you share a home with a person who has PTSD, you might experience some of their suffering and annoyance.

Sometimes you might feel ignored, and other times you might be shocked by your partner's angry outbursts. You might consequently experience a sense of "walking on eggshells."

An unpredictable person may have PTSD, especially if this is a new occurrence. This can put you on your guard and make home life tense.

In some cases, you could develop anxiety over the unexpected, which to some people can be traumatic.

Avoidance
If your partner has unpredictable reactions, you might be overly aware and concerned about upsetting them.

You might start avoiding them or stop talking about specific topics.

Guilt and shame
There are several reasons why you might start feeling guilt or shame when your loved one has PTSD.

You may feel like there was something you could have done to prevent the trauma, or even feel guilty for your health and happiness.

You might opt to isolate yourself from others as a way to support your loved one who isn't ready to socialize. But this can make you feel frustrated or resentful after a while, which can also bring on guilt.

These are natural and valid feelings, but not necessarily true.

You deserve to be well, just like your partner— but although you can't change what happened to them, you can care for them and yourself with the resources that are available to you.

Anger
Anger can come on for many reasons. You may have to take on more household or family responsibilities

now. Or you're faced with a new situation of having to care for your loved one.

It's pretty common to feel overwhelmed and underappreciated when this happens.

Anger can also be a natural response to verbal or physical outbursts, or if your loved one has developed any substance use issues.

Negativity
Your loved one may not appear like the person you know before PTSD. This could make it challenging to retain the same degree of concern or connection you formerly had.

Sometimes, you could feel bad for them since they suddenly don't have the qualities you formerly appreciated.

On the other hand, seeing your loved one suffer and be exposed to unfamiliar situations may also cast a negative light on how you perceive the outside world.

Health Issues
It may be sad and stressful for you as well to see someone you love suffer. Health problems may then result from ongoing stress.

Perhaps your workout and eating habits have altered, or you've started using alcohol or cigarettes as a coping mechanism.

Chronic stress may cause a variety of health issues, such as:

~headaches, migraines, muscle pain, and other physical symptoms
~Issues with sleep
~Numerous factors, including the previously mentioned chronic stress, can contribute to sleep issues.

Your partner's sleeplessness may also be keeping you up at night, and having to sleep in different beds may make you feel distant. You can lay in bed pondering whether your spouse is the source of your stress or worries.

You can develop a persistent sleep disorder if these issues recur often.
There are several ways to restart your sleep cycle. Just keep in mind that supporting your spouse is just as vital as taking care of yourself.

Chapter 3

Loving and connecting with your partner

Post-traumatic stress disorder symptoms may put any relationship to the test. However, recognizing the signs and getting assistance may make both parties' relationships better. Working on the relationship may benefit everyone since social support can aid a person with PTSD.

If a person with PTSD is able to explain what they need from their relationships, having a strong support system may help them get through some of the more challenging PTSD phases. If only you would listen, they would undoubtedly want you to comprehend the following:
1. "We simply want you to listen, rather than continuously attempting to "fix" us."

They may not always want advice given to them. They don't need you to correct them, give them instructions, or judge them against others. Simply staying, sitting with them through the storm, listening, and embracing them is all they need from the ones they love.

2. Please refrain from advising them to "just get over it."

I believe it's fantastic if couples can try to strike a balance between letting someone with PTSD work through their symptoms and also holding their hand to help them recover. I understand that it's terrible to see a loved one suffer, but advising them to "get over it" or making fun of them for their symptoms simply makes the process worse for the person who is really having symptoms. The worst times may be made easier by meeting your spouse where they are and saying things like, "I've got you," "Let me help you breathe," or whatever speaks to them the most.

3. When they go through it, be gentle with them—and yourself.

Don't let it bother you. You undoubtedly have a huge heart, so if you're reading this, you could become upset when your love isn't enough to "heal" someone's PTSD. So keep in mind the following two things: First, despite the fact that many PTSD sufferers may recover, there is no known "cure" for PTSD since there is no way to predict what will cause a relapse in the future. Furthermore, this is not about you. Therefore, be patient with both your spouse and your own heart.

4. To better comprehend what they're going through, think about coming to a therapy session with them.

I believe it is crucial that you accompany your spouse to treatment so the therapist can explain your partner's PTSD to you. I was with my now-husband when I had one of my darkest memories. Despite the fact that I gave him a full explanation of the symptoms of my PTSD and what tends to set them off, he continued to fight with me instead of realizing I was experiencing a flashback. The flashback and the anxiety that followed were greatly worsened by his resistance, and my symptoms persisted for more than a week.

Thankfully, he agreed to accompany me to my next appointment when my therapist recommended it. The therapist was able to explain to my husband in terms he could grasp what I couldn't. Both of them found it to be quite beneficial, and ever since then, whenever I've had symptoms, my husband has always been kind, supporting, and understanding.

5. Recognize that you are not to blame when they are having a poor day.

I hope you realize that it is not your fault if your spouse is having a hard time. For example, if someone are experiencing anything as a result of their PTSD, it is them and not you. Therefore, don't feel guilty if your companion has PTSD-related symptoms such as anxiety.

6. Rather than dismissing our anxieties as "irrational," try to understand them.

The dread that PTSD sufferers encounter may be crippling. One of the easiest ways to alienate someone with PTSD is to attempt to argue with them since this is a dread that often defies reason. Let them speak to you rather than attempting to dissuade them from their anxieties. Pose inquiries. Listen. Let them know you're sympathetic. You just need to recognize that their dread is, in fact, terror; you don't need to comprehend the specifics of it.

7. Find out ways to make them feel secure.

PTSD patients often don't feel secure. You may use your huge heart to your advantage here. You now know some things you can do to make your spouse feel secure since you asked them questions about their anxieties. For some, a hug is the answer. Others may want to see a humorous film. Others find it in a bowl of ice cream, a spontaneous dance party in the kitchen, or a drive through the countryside. Whatever it is, the idea is to let PTSD sufferers know you're there for them along the way rather than trying to fix them.

8. *Recognize that every person deals with the condition in a different manner.*

Every person has their own unique coping mechanisms, which change depending on their personality. I write, for my part. I can better describe how it feels to have PTSD, panic attacks, and despair because to this book.

9. *Don't forget to look for yourself as well.*

I had a sense of disconnection as I worked through my trauma and attempted to manage the intense sensations, emotions, and persistent PTSD symptoms. Prior to developing the abilities to manage my emotions, I felt unhappy, furious, wounded, and in a state of perpetual fear. I interpreted everything my husband said personally and exaggerated everything. I felt raw and exposed, lost all faith in the world, and desperately tried to push him away. I needed regular affirmation that he wasn't leaving me because I was frightened he would do so.

He was shocked, upset, and unsure about how to interact with me going forward. He was confused about what was happening to me, and I'm sure he felt powerless to intervene or fix it. He joined a support group for PTSD partners and began therapy to learn self-care techniques. It's extremely important that our partners get what they need for their own emotional and physical wellbeing.

10. Understand that it's not a day's job

Don't forget you're only human; you cannot fix your partner, to be frank, you cannot even connect so smoothly in a matter of days or weeks. It takes patience and love, lots of it in fact, to be able to break through the barrier they've set to push away human contact or friendship. You don't have to break into an argument when they get too obsessive with what you do, how you do it, and whoever you do it with; you should be prepared knowing that they get insecure. It's okay if they become overly obsessive, it doesn't make your partner a monster, they're just trying to protect you, well, that's what they think. Try not to make them feel stupid or different, just flow with them; laugh about stuff, do anything at all to make them feel secure and happy.

You should even learn to apologize, even when you know you're right, it's really going to take a lot of love for you to really connect with your partner. Never lose sight of why you are doing all of this; it will keep you motivated to go on.

You should also learn to say the words "I Love You" very often. It's true that actions speak louder than words, but that doesn't make the words meaningless.

Chapter 4

Actions to take in order for your relationship to really work

A trauma that happened weeks, months, or even years ago may still be occurring right now for someone with PTSD. No matter when the traumatic incident occurred, it is still occurring for that individual physically and mentally at the time. Despite what your spouse may say, it is time to move on. Someone who hasn't gone through such a tragedy may be surprised when they hear their neighbor pounding noisily on their roof, but they can understand the situation and move on. However, in PTSD sufferers, the body will respond as if it were in danger. It still requires assistance as it tries to make sense of something that is difficult to understand.

Your spouse has to realize that trying to ignore the problem won't make it go away; doing so is merely self-denial and doesn't make a bit of difference.

Additionally, **if you love someone who has PTSD, you too are impacted.** It's important for those who are close to someone with PTSD to look after themselves as well; this is something that is sometimes overlooked, ignored, or rejected. You could be asking yourself, "My spouse experienced that trauma, not me. However, you are also experiencing it to some extent, therefore it is crucial that you take care of yourself.

Don't be too cautious! However, in this situation, exposing your loved one to their sorrow is necessary for the healing process. You may offer to do those errands for your spouse, for instance, if they are anxious when they're in public places with plenty of uncontrollable elements. However, it may be beneficial to learn how to visit such locations and remain there long enough to develop a habit and understand that it is safe to do so. As individuals process their thoughts and emotions around the trauma, there will be some suffering as part of the process.

It may be psychologically and physically draining to be a spouse of someone who has PTSD; take care of yourself, be kind and forgiving to yourself, and schedule time for activities that will help you feel better. Couples counseling, if your spouse is on board, may also be extremely beneficial.

Establish personal boundaries to prevent PTSD from taking control of your life. Living with a person who has PTSD might make you feel as if you have to tread carefully to avoid triggering a stressor. The most effective thing you can do, according to Jain, is to learn how to deal with the symptoms together rather than encouraging or enabling them. Say your spouse suffers from PTSD and as a result, he avoids crowds and refuses to visit the grocery store, parties, or concerts. In many cases, the spouse may promote this behavior in an effort to be supportive by turning down family invites and restricting their own leisure activities in order to accommodate the symptoms. Therefore, nobody moves.

Instead, recognize that this isolation is a sign of PTSD, that therapy is accessible, and that you may still continue to do the activities you like. In the meantime, find a compromise that works for your family.

Being the spouse of someone with post-traumatic stress disorder (PTSD) may be difficult — and irritating — for many reasons. There is nothing that can make you feel as helpless as living with a partner who has PTSD. Although you wish to ease their suffering, you are also struggling with your own guilt about the need of taking care of yourself as well.

You want to know everything, but you often have to accept that this is a condition that cannot be loved out of someone. You may spend years attempting to comprehend how PTSD impacts your spouse, and you could even decide to quit our relationship.Let me tell you right now that it is not and will never be your fault, I may have suffered from PTSD myself but I'm writing this book to te you that you're human and if you eventually walk away, it's not because you didn't love your partner, you did everything you could; how do I know? You're reading a book for your partner's sake! Trust me, you are not a monster, especially if you have done everything you possibly could as a human and as a passionate partner.

How we see the world shapes who we choose to be — and sharing compelling experiences can frame the way we treat each other, for the better. This is a powerful perspective. If your partner can't even try to understand this…..if they can't even try to make an effort to at least make you feel like they know and appreciate what you are doing for them…….then I really don't know what else to say that could help.
I suffered from PTSD too, and I know my husband must have gotten tired at a point, but there were times where I forced myself to actually do something about it,because the truth is, believe it or not, only your partner can truly make the move to become better, and your role is to make them understand that, while giving your full support.
As someone who went through hell and back, here's what I have to say to you, don't give up **easily,** but remember that only you can love yourself more than anyone ever could.
I really hope I was able to help in some way, because the fact that you're reading this book means you really care for your partner,........and if it so happens that no one has said a thank you yet, let me be the first then;
THANK YOU

Don't forget there are significant obstacles when it comes to loving a partner suffering from post-traumatic stress, but there are also threads that come together to create a silver lining. Wishing you a happy relationship with your partner; lots of love, support and prayers from me.

www.ingramcontent.com/pod-product-compliance
Lightning Source LLC
Chambersburg PA
CBHW051941150726
47999CB00006B/2317